MY

SOUL

EXPLODES

MY SOUL EXPLODES

Praise and Meditation Thoughts

The Reverend Dr. Nan M. Brown

Brown Publishing
Post Office Box 39
Kents Store, Virginia 23084

Published by
Brown Publishing
Post Office Box 39
Kents Store, Virginia 23084
E-mail: nmbrown@ceva.net

Cover Design and Logo by
A B Blunt Graphics & Promotional Design
Landover, Maryland 20706

www.xulonpress.com

Thou hast poured oil upon my head, my cup is brimming over;
yes, and all through my life Goodness and Kindness wait on me,
the Eternal's guest, within his household evermore. (TJMB)

MY SOUL EXPLODES

When I take a moment to reminisce about what you've done for me,
How you've brought me every step of the way;
Your guidance, your mercy, your love and forgiveness set me free;
My spirit is filled with thanksgiving and joy that I cannot repay.
My Soul Explodes with thanks!

This life of love, peace, happiness and joy I now have, to you I owe;
This life which is so filled each day;
With joyous work which causes me to grow and grow;
I would not trade how you've blessed me in a marvelous way
My Soul Explodes with thanks!

My cup continues to be filled with your spirit-little by little
with your love;
Until it fills-explodes-and runs over everywhere;
Makes me give continuous thanks to the Father above;
For His compassionate love, concern and wondrous care.
My Soul explodes with thanks!

ACKNOWLEDGMENTS

I am so grateful to acknowledge individuals who have provided me with so much encouragement during the writing of the poems and meditations in this book "MY SOUL EXPLODES" as well as its publication.

For the encouragement, which I received from the members of the Way of the Cross Baptist Church, for which I founded and served as the Pastor for the past fourteen years, I am thankful that you never put stumbling blocks in my paths to interfere with these writings. Now that I have retired as the Pastor, (2003), I still appreciate your encouraging me to continue with the writings which I had begun, but never completed!

To Frank C. Brown, without whose untiring efforts in our home, love, encouragement and support, this book would not have been written and published. Thank you so much.

To Bessie Taylor Jett for unending encouragement, and to Toni Carter Pearson, author of "Joyfully Enter The Temple, Praise and Meditation Starters," for inspiration to get on with "My Soul Explodes," Thank you.

To Virginia Schuyler Waddy, my administrative assistant, for typing the manuscript, I am so grateful.

To Toren Blunt for proofreading the manuscript, thanks so much, Linette Adams, my daughter for her excellent editing capability. Thanks so very much.

Thanks to my children, Alvin, Joseph, Linette, Sami and Ameedah who were a strong source of encouragement and strength during the entire writing and publishing process.

I am especially grateful to Alvin for his graphic design. It is beautiful.

INTRODUCTION

The birth of this book of poems and meditation thoughts is long overdue, mainly because I had not written poems except for special requests from family members or church request for special occasions since I was ten years old. But a few years ago, I began to reminiscence about those early days when I was just a little girl and enjoyed composing poems, and I asked myself the question, "why not now?"

Writing meditations and other script has always come rather easy for me when the situation and surroundings are suitable. Seemingly, I am always comfortable and inspired to write when I visit and/or vacation in a mountainous area. With a little prayer to put myself in the desired mood for writing, the words seem to flow and overflow, and the joy, which comes, is so powerful. So I began to write poems about my family, trees, birds, mountains, or things that I love and whatever inspires me.

When I began to think about a title for such a collection of poems and meditations, I called my daughter to converse with her. When I told her that the poems were my birthing about whatever the spirit put into my mind at the time of writing, and then I mentioned to her a title, which I thought, would be appropriate. My daughter said "Why don't you title the book 'My Soul Explodes,'?" Seems to me that is what happens to you when you begin to write. I thanked her for being so insightful.

And yes, my soul does seem to explode with thoughts and phrases, poem titles, and meditative insights. I am grateful that when I pray and ask God what it is He wants me to write about, He fills my cup until it overflows.

Interestingly enough, my family whom I love dearly brings a

great deal of inspiration for my writing although I choose not to use their names. But I enjoy musing and writing about my spouse, children, grandchildren and great grand children. There are so many tales and stories that I recall. Some have brought joy and inspiration to our family, and others even after the passage of many years, evoke tears and sorrow. Thankfully, we have all grown through these processes—for the better!

I trust that everyone who chooses to read these poems and meditation thoughts in "My Soul Explodes" will be able to identify with and appreciate them. I believe they will give you inspiration and a greater appreciation for life, loving, living and giving.

TABLE OF CONTENTS

THE CARDINAL
(Scriptures)

And to every beast of the earth, and to every
fowl of the air, and to every thing that
creepeth upon the earth, wherein there is
life, I have given every green herb
for meat: and it was so. (Genesis 1:30 KJV)

Be still, and know that I am God: I will
be exalted among the heathen, I will
be exalted in the earth. (Psalm 46:10 KJV)

Finally, my brethren, be strong in the Lord,
and in the power of his might. (Ephesians 6:10 KJV)

THE CARDINAL

Cardinals visit us each year during spring
Their beautiful red and brown color
Lifts my spirit when they "sing"
Cardinals bring joy when they fly around
We know that spring is near when they are on the ground

There's enjoyment to watch them each day
It is significant to watch them as they play
The male cardinal is most beautifully dressed
In his bright red feathers, black beard and his crest

The female cardinal does not have color quite as rich
Her beige and brown feathers are not the red I'd pick
As a color favorite of mine
She's so astute and with her young very kind

Having both male and female cardinals visit our bird feeder
Brings great joy to sit and watch their attentiveness as they are eating
Their consideration of each other will draw attention
To see this take place is surely worth the mention

Through him then let us continually offer up a
sacrifice of praise to God,
That is, the fruit of lips that acknowledges his name.
(Hebrews 13: 15 RSV)

THE GARDEN

The garden is a place where the gracefulness of
God is seen
The growing vegetables are beautiful and green
The much needed rain has come and gone
It is amazing to see now how everything has grown

The greens left after last winter's snow
Have taken on new life as never before
There's leafy kale and healthy collard greens
And even now the swiss chard can be seen

The broccoli plants, which were recently set out
Are growing fast from the release of the drought
And today the sun is as bright as can be
The whole garden is shouting for the victory

The strawberries, which appeared to be without life
Have spread their leaves and their vines cried out
"Oh! I give praise to the one above"
Who has given us new warmth and extended love

The onion plants are beginning to peep up
They are like happy "waggle" – tailed pups
Swaying back and forth as the wind's breezes blow
Now that the sunshine is bright, they are ready to grow

The green peas, beans, beets, carrots and such
Are just waiting for "their time" to come up
They have just soaked up the rain in their seeds
Just a few more days and they too will change in the breeze

The garden is surely a great gift from God
It provides so much good food from the clods
Food that's provided by God's mercy and grace
That we humans must always give Him the praise

The Earth (Scriptures)

*O Lord, our Lord, how majestic is thy name in all the earth!
Thou whose glory above the heavens is chanted by the mouth
of babes and infants, thou hath founded a bulwark because of
thy foes, to still the enemy and the avenger. When I look at thy
heavens, the work of thy fingers, the moon and the stars which
thou hast established; what is man that thou are mindful of
him, and the son of man that thou dost care for him?
Yet thou hast made him little less than God, and dost
crown him with glory and honor. Thou hast given him dominion
over the works of thy hands; thou hast put all things under his feet,
all sheep and oxen, and also the beasts of the field, the birds of the
air, and the fish of the sea, whatever passes along the paths of
the sea. O Lord, our Lord, how majestic is thy name in all the earth!*
(Psalm 8: 1-9 RSV)

*Make a joyful noise to the Lord, all the earth; break forth into
joyous song and sing praises! Sing praises to the Lord with the
lyre, with the lyre and the sound of melody! With trumpets and the
sound of the horn make a joyful noise before the King, the Lord!
Let the sea roar, and all that fills it, the world and those who dwell
in it! Let the floods clap their hands; let the hills sing for joy
together before the Lord, for he comes to judge the earth. He will
judge the world with righteousness, and the peoples with equity.*
(Psalm 98:4-9 RSV)

THE EARTH

I saw a big round yellow circle last night
The sky was filled with twinkling stars
What a gorgeous and astounding sight
To become aware of how God makes
Everything so bright
The earth speaks to me!

As I sat in my car to drive
Locked my seat belt around my side
Began to drive down the winding road
Rabbits, deer families, even a toad
Free to graze and play in the fields in the dark
There are no hunters, or dogs to bark
These animals come out at night to eat
They run, play and do not sleep

It is winter, and we are very aware
There is snow and ice everywhere
The tree limbs are all covered with ice
They look like gleaming Christmas tree lights
Heavy from the frozen water weight
The earth just holds a steady gait
The earth speaks to me!

People who do not have a second heating source
Find it difficult to manage to keep warm, of course
Their food becomes in short supply
Much is lost with so much sleet and ice
The earth speaks to me!

The earth lets us know that it is winter
Cold, cold, and low temperatures are sinister
Now and then we experience a few days of spring
The birds come back and begin to sing
The earth speaks to me!

About three more weeks before spring begins
As I look around now there are buds on some things
The yellow from forsythia is beautiful and bright
I begin to realize that warm weather is in sight
A few more days and spring will come
Then there will be warmer days from the sun
The earth speaks to me!

If I were hungry, I would not tell you; for the world and all that is in it is mine.

(Psalm 50:12 RSV)

But about midnight Paul and Silas were praying and singing hymns to God, and the prisoners were listening to them, and suddenly there was a great earthquake, so that the foundations of the prison were shaken, and immediately all the doors were opened and every one's fetters were unfastened. When the jailer woke and saw that the prison doors were open; he drew his sword and was about to kill himself, supposing that the prisoners had escaped. But Paul cried with a loud voice, "Do not harm yourself, for we are all here." And he called for lights and rushed in, and trembling with fear he fell down before Paul and Silas, and brought them out and said, "Men, what must I do to be saved?" And they said, "Believe in the Lord Jesus, and you will be saved, you and your household."

(Acts 16: 25-31 RSV)

THE EARTH TREMBLES

There is a fault in Columbia I'm told
We'd lived in this area nearly twenty years
And yes, a few trembles I had felt
Never shared this information, sort of kept it to myself

But then one bright sunny day in my bathroom I sat
There was rather a great tremble of the earth
The sound was like that of a train filled with freight
Our entire house began for a spell to shake
At first I thought it was a jet plane

When we are afraid or unaware
We try to find somebody with whom we share

From my bathroom to the kitchen I ran fast
Like the deer sometimes I see in the grass
"What was that?" I asked my spouse
He looked more frightened than a little gray mouse
"I don't know," he responded to me
Could have been an earthquake you see

Let me call 911 to ask if they know what has been done
I felt rather "sick" with fear, no pun
"Did we just have an earthquake, I inquired?"
"Not sure, but we think so," he replied.

The waters swelled and increased greatly on the earth;
and the ark floated on the face of the waters. The waters
swelled so mightily on the earth that all the high mountains
under the whole heaven were covered; the waters swelled
above the mountains, covering them fifteen cubits deep.
(Genesis 7: 18-20 NRSV)

Let the floods clap their hands; let the hills sing together for joy.
(Psalms 98:8 NRSV)

When Jesus had come down from the mountain,
great crowds followed him.
(Matthew 8: 1 NRSV)

THE MOUNTAINS

Mountains have always intrigued me
They cause my mind to wonder, how they came to be
With their awesome peaks, and valleys below
Their rocks, trill, and vegetation that grows

There is no doubt that they were all in God's plan
They surely caused much philosophizing by man
Trying to fathom just how and from whence they came
Was it in the "big bang," or was it just by God's name

Did God just speak and mountains come into place?
Or was it His almighty power and grace?
Did God point his index finger and they rose from the sea?
Are these thoughts there just to puzzle you and me?

I am sure the scientist would say they know
Why mountains stand so high with valleys below
But their findings have not sufficiently brought
Answers that cause silence to my thoughts

I want the mountains to speak for themselves
As if they were some tiny fairy tale elves
Give me some answers about how you came to be
With vegetation growing between, in spite of the rocks I see
Colors more beautiful than the rainbow-orange, greens and reds-
Keep a myriad of thoughts still dancing in my head

The sun shall no more be your light by day,
nor shall the moon shed light on you, but
your unending light shall be the Eternal, your
God shall be your splendour.
(Isaiah 60:19 TJMB)

THE SUN

Today I see an orange glow in the light blue sky
The sun begins to peep up over the horizon
What a great difference the sun makes in my day
Blessings, blessing just to watch it rise
And makes its way up in the glorious sky

The brightness of the sun gives the great joy
It takes away my feelings of depression
I feel added strength, energy and Oh boy!
Now, I loose the fear of oppression
Blessings, blessing just to watch it rise

…You can rest unafraid, you can lie down to a sweet sleep;
never need you fear sudden lows or the storm
that strikes the wicked,
for the Eternal will be your protection,
and preserve you from all danger.
(Proverbs 3: 24-26 TJMB)

THE STORMS

Storms have always caused me concern
As a child, we were told "You must be quiet and still"
During a storm my heart would seem to burn
We were afraid we were in for a kill

What with lightening streaking
And thunder so loud causing things to shake
The whole house would be squeaking
Wind blew so hard we thought everything would break

During these storms we would gather and pray
Plead with God to send rain quick
Seemed when rain really would spray
The thunder and lightening would soon quit

We remember one storm in our life
As we sat in the living room of our house
It thundered hard and lightened simultaneously
A big red-yellowish ball came through the screen
And rolled through the room as quiet as a mouse

We were all stunned and sat very still
Fear gripped us all and we were afraid
We began to feel very, very ill
We thought we might be struck by the red-yellowish ball
That was ahead

We all thanked God for mercy and Grace
And we prayed for a safe place
God heard and answered our prayer
And very soon we knew His spirit was there

He is like a tree planted by a stream,
that bears fruit in due season, with leaves that never fade;
whatever he does, he prospers.
(Psalm 1:3 TJMB)

THE TREES

Trees bring so much beauty
So many different kinds
Palms, poplars, white oaks
Maples, black oaks, cedars and pines

Trees bring so much beauty
In many different colors, Greens-
Light, dark, Kelley, and dark lime
Their beauty speaks to our spirits all of the time

Trees bring so much beauty
Wood for beautiful homes where we can rest
Wood for fire to keep us warm
A place where animals can nest

Trees bring so much beauty
Fruits that have good taste that help with our health
Trees provide medicines to help diseases subside
And miracles of unexpected wealth

He sacrificed also and burnt incense in the high places,
and on the hills, and under every green tree.
(II Chronicles 28:4 KJV)

For a good tree bringeth not forth corrupt fruit;
neither doth a corrupt tree bring forth good fruit.
For every tree is known by his own fruit. For
of thorns men do not gather figs, not of a
bramble bush gather they grapes
(Luke 6:43-44 KJV)

A TREE

A tree is such a magnificent gift to man
Its leaves and branches provide for all of his clan
Cool breeze and shade from the summer heat
Flowering beauty in spring that one cannot beat
A kaleidoscope of colors God gives in the fall
Reds, yellows, oranges, and greens standing tall
Then winter comes and things look bleak
But the tree is still just asleep
When it awakens and buds in spring
It is no wonder that nature begins to sing!

And out of the ground made the Lord God to grow every tree
that is pleasant to the sight, and good for food;....
(Genesis 1:9b)

THE WALNUT TREE

I have observed the walnut tree
With its lofty branches filled with nuts
I ask myself, "How old can it be?"
   It stands so tall, there's no way I could ever touch

Its top that spans many years of time
   Its grayish-brown bark is sturdy and firm
   If I were a little younger, I 'd try to climb
   All the way to the top without one squirm

To see what earth looks like below
   I'd love to grab a few walnuts along the way
   And feel the cool breeze of the wind as it blows
To provide coolness to my sweating face

Oh! If only this walnut tree could speak
   The words that one might hear first might be
"Thank you God for making me a tree."
   I try to be fruitful, but I am about to thirst
For you have held back the rain
   When you create again please let me be
   Something other than a Black Walnut Tree

I don't want to sound ungrateful to you God
For you are always giving whatever we need
And I really thank you from the depths of my heart
For the carbon monoxide that I breathe

Thank you for the walnuts you help me to grow
    Almost everybody loves them because of such great taste
Especially the brownie lovers, you know
    They eat them as if no crumbs, can they waste

Thank you God for creating me
I am the Black Walnut Tree

Note: This poem was written as I sat in the car on a steamy hot day waiting for my Administrative Assistant to complete her doctor's visit in Goochland County, Virginia, under a very, very old black walnut tree, August 2002.

For my soul is full of troubles,
and my life draws near to Sheol.
(Psalm 88:3 NRSV)

And God, who searches the heart, knows what is
the mind of the Spirit, because the Spirit intercedes
for the saints according to the will of God.
(Romans 8:27 NRSV)

SUMMER WITHIN

It seems that winter is trying desperately to invade my soul
When right now I need the bright colored flowers of summer
As the cool breeze blows over the flowers, and their fragrance
Eases the pain of my loss and my sorrow
I try to open my hands and my nostrils wide, wide to grasp
And smell the spirit that God has sprayed in the air—
The aliveness, the joy, the love, the peace and all of
The fragrance that tends to push winter away as the winter's
Grayness tries to invade my invincible soul.

I remember his longing half opened longing eyes, his gray mustache his
Balding head, his deep rattled breathing, his struggle for each breath
His longing eyes seemed to be saying "Nan, please do something for
Me." But what could I do? Death was already slowly taking him away.
Yes, winter is trying desperately to invade his soul and mine.
When right now, we need the beautiful blue sky without the clouds to
Provide a sense of love, peace and oneness with the eternal—
To keep my summer within and send winter into a long distant orbit
That it will not return—

I long for the beauty of summer right now—to take away my grief—
To brighten my day with the gleaming brightness and light of the sun;
Winter is so bleak, snowy, cold, steady rains that dampen the earth and
 Cause so much joint pain.
Winter nights are spread out long like a curtain—darkness, dreams of
Those whose lives were snuffed out long ago, and bringing to mind the
Brevity of life with all its disappointments.

I prefer the warmth of summer rather than the extreme cold of
December and January when death seems to come oh, so frequently—
It's as if the years do not wish to go out alone—It's as if they ask "Who
Can we take with us before year's end?" God, please give me summer
Within! Beautiful green grass spread out like a blanket—flowers—
Yellow, purple, red, orange, pink and green—fill me with their
Fragrance love, joy, peace, —for myself and
for all those I love so much
Please give us today, summer within!

They have mouths, but do not speak, eyes, but do not see.
(Psalms 115:5 RSV)
Redeeming the time, because the days are evil.
(Ephesians 5:16 KJV)

DRIVING THROUGH THE RAIN

Windy, cold, rainy day!
Trying so hard to see my way
  Big tractor-trailers spraying rain everywhere
Not very much visibility out there

  Many cars, no lights, all driving very fast
  Speeding on the Interstate—Hum! We might not last
To reach with safety our destination
  So I began to pray quietly without hesitation

  God, your outstanding protection we surely need
To face this traffic who has no creed
  They drive like batmen in video games
Zigzagging in and out of all the lanes

So sad, most, no signals they give
  Just dart in and out—don't care if they die or live
  At least that's the way it seems to me
Maybe I'm just scared due to lack of visibility

  But God, please hear my earnest prayer
  And protect us from danger with your utmost care
  Please shackle my nerves and ease my pain
And help us to make it home safely in this windy, cold, rain

God Almighty must have heard my sincere prayers
I know he is a mighty God and he is everywhere
He answered my prayer even in my fear
We arrived home safely even through my tears

(Hum! I'm tired and worn out! And I wasn't even driving—my husband was.)

For I know the plans I have for you, says the Lord.
"They are plans for good and not for disaster,
to give you a future and a hope."
(Jeremiah 29:11 NLT)

You have turned my mourning into joyful dancing.
You have taken away my clothes of mourning
and clothed me with joy.
(Psalm 30:11 NLT)

In one of the villages,
Jesus met a man with an advanced case of leprosy.
When the man saw Jesus, he fell to the ground,
face down in the dust, begging to be healed.
"Lord," he said, "If you want to, you can make
me well again." Jesus reached out and touched the man.
"I want to," he said, "Be healed!"
And instantly the leprosy disappeared.
(Luke 5:12-13 NLT)

THE WAVES

Are there waves in your life this New Years Day
That ripple and splash and swell
Waves that bring tears of sadness come what may
And leave us drained, limp and we cannot tell

The secrets of our aching hearts, our constant pains and hurts
These waves just continue to bob us up and down
And we try to ride each one as they flip us over with their jerks
And although as hard as we may try, we cannot hide the frowns

But my child get a hold of yourself this New Years Day
For you are not ever lost or alone with your waves
God sends his ministering Angels to wipe your tears away
So you can tenaciously hold on no matter how much your life sways

*My eager desire and hope being that I may never feel ashamed,
but that now as ever I may do honour to Christ in my
own person by fearless courage.
(Philippians 1:20 JMB)*

NO SHAME

Yes, my eager desire and hope was that I would never feel ashamed to honor or worship Jesus my Savior. But years ago, I was ashamed to really recognize the power and presence of what I know now as the Holy Spirit. But on New Year's Day in the year of our Lord 1998, I wrote the following words in my journal for that day:

"New Year's Day—Oh! I do recall when I was ashamed of My Christ, but not since I accepted the call of His voice to go preach the Good News! Thank God, I did 'shut out every other consideration." To be His alone and now I am no longer ashamed. For He touched me, filled me, chose me and sent me to preach and Pastor three different churches. What a joy has filled my soul! Oh yes! "Something happened, and now I know, He touched me and made me whole."

Today, it's been more than twenty years and I have not turned back. Thank God for the courage.

Paul's writings in Philippians tell us of his determination that nothing would deter him from doing exactly what God wanted him to do. God had to stir me up to get me to preach. It was not my choice at the time of the first call. And yes, I posed many questions to Him before he presented me with a providential crisis where there was nothing for me to do but to give an unequivocal yes!

NMB

THE HOLY SPIRIT
(Scriptures)

*Moreover the spirit lifted me up, and brought me unto the
East gate of the Lord's house, which looketh eastward, and behold
At the door of the gate five and twenty men; among whom I
Saw Jaazaniah the son of Azur, and Pelatiah the son of
Benaiah, princes of the people.
(Ezekiel 11:1 KJV)*

*And John was clothed with camel's hair, and with a girdle of a
Skin about his loins and he did eat locusts
and wild honey; and preached,
Saying, there cometh one mightier than
I after me, the latchet of whose
Shoes I am not worthy to stoop down and unloose.
(Mark 1:6-7 KJV)*

*For the Holy Ghost I shall teach you in the same hour
what ye ought to say.
(Luke 12:12 KJV)*

*The Spirit of the Lord is upon me, because he hath anointed me to
preach the gospel to the poor; he hath sent me to heal the
broken-hearted, to preach deliverance to the captives, and
recovering of sight to the blind, to set at liberty
them that are bruised.
(Luke 4:18KJV)*

THE HOLY SPIRIT

I remember well the day I stood
In front of the church as anyone could
And God put a prayer deep in my heart
For my procrastination had long played a part
In preventing me from accepting the call
To preach God's word which for years I had stalled

For most of my life I had struggled with inward fear
Each time the third part of The Trinity came near
Even in my youth I wanted no one to know
That the Holy Spirit affected my own spirit so
There was a difference in me,
family and friends failed to understand
Lots of space and time alone, needed to be away from the clan
To pour out of the depths of my soul to God
Secrets that others knew not how I trod
Over pathways only known to me as He inspired
And set my soul over and over on celestial fire

I did not know early on what the heat came from
But later I realized it came from the Father and the Son
So here I stand praying in the church
Without boldness, but humility and a new birth
For when the Holy Spirit moved across my back
The warmth from its fire was certainly no match
For what Christians felt on the day of Pentecost
When the followers knew the risen Jesus Christ had died on the cross
So this essential gift of the Holy Spirit came
To bring assurance of the promise in His name

Then as I began to pray aloud
A great stir began among the crowd
The Holy Spirit was such a great encompassing power
That I prayed for what seemed like an hour
I promised God I would answer His relentless call
To teach and preach the Gospel resting
On his promise that I could not fall
All of the burdens previously felt were lifted
And I knew undoubtedly that I had been gifted
By none other than the Father and Son above
As long as I continued in his obedience and love

So when I felt that warmth from the Holy Spirit's flame
I knew without a doubt it was God who called my name
It took only a few minutes to answer
Lord, I will go, send me with utmost speed
To teach and preach throughout the whole world
Wherever your Holy Spirit shall lead.

And he hath put a new song in my mouth, even praise unto our
God; many shall see it, and fear, and shall trust in the Lord.
(Psalm 40:3 KJV)

I will praise thee, O Lord, among the people; and I will
sing praises unto thee among the nations. For thy mercy is
great above the heavens: and thy truth reacheth unto the clouds.
(Psalm 108:3-4 KJV)

Then again called they the man that was blind, and said unto him.
Give God the praise;
we know that this man is a sinner. He answered
And said, whether he be a sinner or no, I know not; one thing
I know, that, whereas I was blind, now I see.
(John 9:24-25 KJV)

THE HIGHEST PRAISE

Today God we give you the highest praise
You are so worthy because without you
We could not have been raised
From all of our sin and degradation
You have brought us to the light of emancipation
So, we give you the highest praise!

You have awakened us to a day brand new
Filled with so many interesting things to do
Thank you for filling our mind and hearts
So we may realize that we all have a significant part
So, we give you the highest praise!

A part to play that's filled with your matchless love
For all that we greet on the journey toward the above
As pilgrims traveling toward your light
Keeping you as our centered focus both day and night
So, we give you the highest praise!

As pilgrims on this journey below
We experience so much joy in our lives as we continue to grow
Each day as we strive to become more and more like you
As we stretch our hands to others as you commanded us to do
So, we give you the highest praise!

We realize our praise and thanks are never enough
To reimburse you for your kindness and generosity to us
For paying that great price on Calvary
That a sinner like me could be set free
So, we give you the highest praise!

Today we surrender ourselves totally to thee
To be used in your divine work graciously
That we may bring others from over the land
Into your mighty salvation plan
So, we give you the highest praise!

Be subject to one another, from reverence for Christ.
Wives be subject to your husband as the Lord,
For the husband is the head of the wife as Christ also
(Though he is the Savior of the Body) is the head of the church;
as the church is subject to Christ,
so wives are to be subject to their husbands in every respect.
Husbands love your wives as Christ loved the church
And gave Himself up for her...
(Ephesians 5:21-26, TJMB)

THE CHURCH

The church is a marvelous institution
It is a place where we can gain spirituality
Founded by the highest power
It is a place where we learn about eternity

The church is where we can congregate
A place where we meet loved ones and friends
It is a place where we can escape
All of our aloneness that we tend to bring in

The Church is a place where we can kneel and pray
About all of the misery we may bring in
It's a place where we can be alleviated
Of the frustrations and disappointments of our sins

The church is a place where beautiful music we hear
To stir a great spirit of our souls within
Inspired by true words preached as we come near
Added strength and empowerment to our minds again

Do your best to present yourself to God as one approved,
a workman who has no need to be ashamed,
rightly handling the word of truth.
(II Timothy 2:15 RSV)

But as for you, teach what befits sound doctrine.
(Titus 2:1 RSV)

And the gospel must first be preached to all nations.
(Mark 13:10 RSV)

THE BIBLE

The Bible is the greatest book ever written
It is filled with living instructions and great wisdom
It, must be read, studied, meditated upon well
To do this will help to keep you from the fires of hell

The Bible is a treasure filled with how we should live
Its contents are breathed with the best God chose to give
As guidance for our lives one day at a time
It is given and inspired by the Holy Spirit divine

Reading the Bible provides great inspiration
It teaches us from the beginning all about creation
It provides us with so many open doors
That we can walk through more and more

Then the other administrators and princes began searching
for some fault in the way Daniel was handling his affairs,
but they couldn't find anything to criticize. He was faithful
and honest and always responsible.
(Daniel 6:4NLT)

Long ago God spoke many times and in many ways
to our ancestors through the prophets.
(Hebrews 1:1 NLT)

They replied, "Believe on the Lord Jesus and you will be saved,
along with your entire household."
(Acts 16:31 NLT)

MY FAITH

I am grateful that I have received
The gift of faith that enables me to believe
In a God who is full of mercy and grace
Who always sticks by me no matter what I face
My Faith!

Some days when my faith gets a little weak
And the trials and tribulations almost knock me off my feet
I know that I must hang in there
And I'm able to do that through constant prayer
My Faith!

During these times when life deals such a blow
I lean heavily on the Word of God in order to forgo
The human tendency in our pity to weep
Without the thought He continually intercedes
And we really have it made
My Faith!

Rise during the night and cry out. Pour out your hearts like
water to the Lord. Lift up your hands to him in prayer.
Plead for your children as they faint with hunger in the streets.
(Lamentations 2:19 NLT)

One day soon afterward Jesus went to a mountain
to pray, and he prayed to God all night.
(Luke 6:12 NLT)

Keep alert and pray. Otherwise temptation will overpower you.
For though the spirit is willing enough, the body is weak
(Matthew 26:41 KJV)

BEGINNING MY DAY
WITH PRAYER

It's great to begin the day with prayer
Just take the time to let God know you care
Give thanks for just being awakened
Praise for health, wisdom, happiness and strength
About family, friends, and His creation

Pray for those troubled persons who have asked for your prayers
Persons who are burdened with bodies filled with disease
Whose doctors have told them there is no cure
Pray for their healing and wholeness please
That only God can enable them to endure

Pray for our world and its stability
For people who are unemployed and homeless and no security
For persons who are hungry and without proper food
For their surroundings that keep them in terrible moods

And then don't forget to pray for yourself
Ask God to give you guidance for the day
To do what would be pleasing to Him in every way
As you begin your prayer for that day
Pray and expect answer for them

How hast thou counseled him that hath no wisdom?
And how hast thou plentifully declared the things as it is?
To whom hast thou uttered words?
And whose spirit came from thee?
(Job 26:3-4 KJV)

Let the redeemed of the Lord say so, whom he hath
redeemed from the hand of the enemy.
(Psalm 107: 2 KJV)

GOD'S SONG IN MY HEART

Thank you God for the song in my heart
It's dear to me because it comes from you
This song is about his assurance on my part
A song in my soul about Jesus keeps me from being blue

Thank you God for the song in my soul
A song that feeds me day and night
Because your love and glory are so bold
They shine all around me so bright

Thank you God for the song in my spirit
That warms my heart and mind
Your song in my heart brings joy to hear it
Your song O God is like sight to the blind

Thank you God for your song gives life
It's so beautiful, and filled with love
Your song in my heart is a song about Christ
It's a song of love from heaven above

God help us to sing your song always
For they give energy, strength, and fire
Help me to continue to show your Praise
To keep your song in my heart shall always be my desire

Pray at all times in the Spirit, with all prayer
and supplication. To that end keep alert with
all perseverance, making supplication
for all the saints.
(Ephesians 6:18 RSV)

GOD'S LOVE IS OVER EVERY CREATURE

A few years ago, I had the privilege of visiting the sunny, beautiful, flower land of Zimbabwe, and of attending the first All-Africa Assembly of The Baptist World Alliance. Living conditions for many in Zimbabwe were surely not the best. But what great joy it was to meet and fellowship with such loving and caring Christians. While there, I preached for several congregations. The most impressive part of these worship services was the prayer time. What a moving experience it was to see these Christians, who were so much in need themselves, pour out their hearts in prayer and supplication for their brothers and sisters in other lands. It really exemplified their sincere love.

If we are to be strong in the Lord, we need to put on the whole armor of God, lest we forget whose we are! As we pray at all time in the spirit, let us remember to make supplications for our brothers and sisters whom Christ commanded us to love, all over the world.

O Lord, whose love is over every creature, help us to love and care enough about our brothers and sisters around the world that we remember them daily in our prayers. Amen

But ye are a chosen race, a royal priesthood, a holy nation,
God's own people, that you may declare the wonderful
deeds of him who called you out of darkness
into his marvelous light.
(1 Peter 2: 9 KJV)

GOD'S LOVE FOR US

Like many persons, I suspect that there have been many days in my life when I have felt unloved by those with which I have lived among or came into contact. Individuals have unique ways of letting others know when they are looked down upon or not appreciated. Some are very subtle, while others are open and hostile.

There were days I would arrive home from the office feeling listless and drained. Not as much from the work in which I was engaged, as the stress and strain of being in the company of co-workers who seemed to experience great joy in putting others down. But upon reading this verse of Scripture, I would be comforted and would remember that we are all God's children-cared for, loved deeply by Him, and belonging to God.

Belonging to God because of His great love for us has named us a royal priesthood to serve the King of kings. When God names us, no one can cause us to lose our identity. We can stand ten feet tall. With joy in our souls, we can proclaim that we are a part of the household of God. No amount of persecution can drown out God's call or his love for us. No amount of self-pity will ever make God stop calling or loving us.

Dear God, we thank you for having chosen and called us, because you loved us so much. Kindle within our souls a holy flame so that we may boldly proclaim the blessedness of your kingdom far and near. Amen

But He said to me. My grace is sufficient for you,
for my power is made perfect in weakness....
(II Cor. 12:9a RSV)

THE GRACE OF A LOVING GOD

There is no doubt in my mind that God is a loving God who willingly dispenses His grace in our behalf. A few years ago, I was driving to church, and a truck with the license tags "Hey 20" was in front of me, but the driver was driving more slowly than I wanted to travel. I had been delayed in leaving home because of a telephone call. I really wanted to drive much faster so as not to be so late in getting to church. But to my surprise, the driver of the truck seemed to have slowed down even more so. I really wanted to pass him, but the drive to the church is almost all in no passing zones. The Holy Spirit did not lead me to try to pass, so I stayed behind the slow-moving truck. It is amazing how God showers his grace on us even when we don't deserve it. Just about halfway from the church the truck slowed to even a slower pace and came to almost a complete stop. Needless to say, I was even more disgusted until I looked more closely in front of the truck. He had stopped to let a family of deer cross the road.

Had I passed the truck and sped onward, surely I would have had an accident, and possibly been killed or maimed. But because of God's loving grace, this did not happen.

The Apostle Paul was rather impatient about his illness too. Three times he prayed that God would remove the thorn in his flesh, but God reminded him that His grace was sufficient for Him.

God's loving grace is available to all of us. We just need to accept it. For Christ's sake we can be content with weaknesses, calamities, and become more patient knowing Christ's love and grace makes us strong when we are weak.

O God of mercy, love and grace, I thank you today for your ministering spirits, my guardian angel, who you sent ahead of me to protect me and save me from myself, Lord, help us to have the patience to wait on Thee always. AMEN.

And the multitudes asked him, "What then shall we do?"
And He answered them, "He who has two coats,
let him share with him who has none;
and he who has food, let him do likewise."
(Luke 3: 10-11 RSV)

SHARING OUR BLESSINGS
WITH LOVE

In its way, the children's movie some years ago "Care Bears" was a much needed film. Our children need to be reminded of the importance of showing love and concern for others. Perhaps many have forgotten how to do that.

It may be well for us to ask the question which the multitudes posed to John the Baptist, "What then shall we do?" We are perplexed today too. We listen, but do not understand, John's answer was one of caring and sharing- a social gospel, if you like.

Discrimination and cries of hunger from our brothers and sisters around the world call out to us. It is a tragedy that we do not hear until a catastrophic sense of urgency awakens us to the needs of others. Because we know and experience God's care and love for us, it is through us that all in need, should experience that same love.

The gospel writer, John, makes it clear for us as he tells us "For God so loved the world that He gave His only begotten son that whosoever believeth in Him should not perish, but have everlasting life." (John 3:16) There is no greater gift of love than this!

O God, without your caring and love, what would we do? Help us to be caring, loving and to share our blessings with our brothers and sisters all over the world. Amen

And their eyes were opened; and Jesus straitly charged them,
saying; see that no man know it.
I will lift up mine eyes unto the hills, from whence cometh my help.
(Matthew 9:30, Psalm 121:1 KJV)

THANK GOD FOR EYES

Eyes are such a precious body part
It is so wonderful to have eyes to see
As I look out toward the mountain
I see and hear two crows as they "caw"
To each other I believe they speak
They seem to be very happy indeed

Without eyes it would be difficult to see
The beauty of the lights of the fireflies
As they flit about from place to place magnificently
Their occasional lights add beauty, and
A sense of great peace to our lives

Without eyes it would be difficult for us to find our way
We would be stumbling, falling and breaking bones
Our ways would not be so steady or easy to take
There probably would be lots of groans

Without eyes we would miss the orange glow of the sunset
This would cause irritability and regrets
Without eyes we would not be able to see
Our beautiful children, grandchildren and great grands
Without our eyes we'd have to depend on someone else's hands

Thank you, God for giving us eyes
Blindness would be depressing to me
So whenever we are giving thankfulness and praise
We must remember to give you thanks
For our spiritual eyesight through which your face we see

JUST THINKING
(Scriptures)

O God, you are my God, I seek you, my soul thirsts for you;
my flesh faints for you, as in a dry and weary land
where there is no water.
So I have looked upon you in the sanctuary,
beholding your power and glory.
Because your steadfast love is better than life,
my lips will praise you.
So I will bless you as long as I live,
I will lift up my hands and call
on you name.(Psalm 63:1-4 NRSV)

So we can say with confidence, "The Lord is my helper;
I will not be afraid. What can anyone do to me?"
(Hebrews 13:6 NRSV)

JUST THINKING

There is peace;
Love,
Joy!

There is patience;
Listening,
Justice!

There is promise;
Light,
Living!

There is practice;
Life,
Giving!

There is persistence;
Lasting,
Strong!

There is thanksgiving;
Praise,
Happiness,
Song!

There is wisdom;
Knowledge,
Grace!

There is strength;
Flight,
Soaring!

There is protection;
Fearlessness,
Power,
Knowing!

There is celebration;
Laughter,
Love!

And always help from
The God above.

The Lord bless you and keep you; the Lord make his face to shine upon you, and be gracious to you; the Lord lift up his countenance upon you, and give you peace. So they shall put my name on the Israelites, and I will bless them.
(Numbers 6:24-27 NRSV)

For with you is the fountain of life; in your light we see light.
(Psalms 36:9 NRSV)

THE POWER OF A SMILE

When I awoke early this morning, I thanked God above
For giving me a most gracious gift from the bounty of His love
It is a gift that inspires extraordinary warmth and grace
By those who are willing to put a big, wide smile upon their face

Yes, bright, white gleaming teeth radiate so much power
When a smile adorns the faces in the early morning hours
Waking for some in the morning does not warrant a smile
But I contend that it is this phenomenon that makes life worthwhile

It takes so much effort to frown than to smile
The power of a genuine smile alleviates stress and keeps you in style
So why not try to take the lines out of your face
And be sure to smile when you are confronted with this grace

There are so many things that a beautiful smile can do
Just try it and you will have to agree with this truth
That a smile can brighten someone's unhappy day
And fill them with joy all along life's way

A smile can cheer you up when you would otherwise be blue
It can give you that energy to enable you to break through
The dreary cloudiness of a cold, windy, winter day
And fill your heart with words of love when you kneel down to pray

Behold, what manner of love the Father hath bestowed upon us,
that we should be called the sons of God: therefore the world
knoweth us not, because it knew him not. Beloved,
now are we the sons of God, and it doth not yet appear
what we shall be but we know that,
when he shall appear, we shall be like him;
for we shall see him as he is.
(I John 3:1-2 KJV)

For God so loved the world, that he gave his only begotten Son,
that whosoever believeth in him should not perish,
but have everlasting life.
(John 3:16 KJV)

LOVE

Love is such a strong force
Its power is as energetic as can be
Love always keeps me on the right course
Even when I am wavering unintentionally

Love is powered from holding on to God's hand
God's love is patient, strong, forgiving and kind
Without His love we could not stand
Praise God for His love is not shallow like yours and mine

That is why to God I always try to cling
I pray for His love, never to leave me alone
It is God's everlasting love about which I daily sing
As I go about my everyday chores at home

Blessed are they that keep his testimonies
and that seek him with the whole heart.
(Psalms 119:2 KJV)

HAPPINESS

When I think about the creation
The world, the mountains, rivers and streams
It's so good to give Praise to our God
For his blessings of love to us
Without shriek or scream

The purple mountains are so glorious and awesome
We think questionably about their formulation
They make us wonder about such beauty
And how the mountainess soil supports vegetation

Yes, the mountains give us much peace and happiness
They help us to focus on God's extensiveness
The mountains tend to put a smile on our face
They bring happiness and smiles that we must embrace

The Spirit of the Lord God is upon me; because the Lord
hath anointed me to preach good tidings unto the meek;
he hath sent me to bind up the brokenhearted,
to proclaim liberty to the captives, and the opening
of the prison to them that are bound.
(Isaiah 61:1 KJV)

A merry heart doeth good like a medicine:
but a broken spirit drieth the bones.
(Proverbs 17:22 KJV)

These things have I spoken unto you,
that my joy might remain in you,
and that your joy might be full.
(John 15:11 KJV)

COUNT IT ALL JOY!

Do you ever get frustrated when family and friends
try to put you down?
What I'm about to recommend is hard to do without a frown
Rejoice and be exceedingly glad in your heart
For God had heard your prayers right from the start
Count It All Joy!

Do you ever feel appreciation—-deprivation?
By family and friends who never give you a deserved commendation?
By whom instead you are thoughtlessly criticized
When words of sincere appreciation
And encouragement should be itemized?
Count It All Joy!

Do you ever love someone who does not know how to love?
Who because of their upbringing in a family who never hugged
Does not know how their love to express
Nor how to give love at its very best
Count It All Joy!

Do you ever feel lonely and very sad
Because you miss the love that you should have had
But your mate does not even seem to be aware
That your needs are all wrapped up in his inability to just care
Count It All Joy!

Remember, your father knows how you feel
He will step in, and he can certainly heal
The sadness you experience that makes you cry
All of the tears from your eyes he will certainly dry
Then you can Count It All Joy!

He will give you joy for each new day
But you must trust him and be able to say
My God, I surrender my total self to you
And I know that you will always be here for me too
Now, I can Count It All Joy!

For the wages of sin is death,
but the free gift of God is eternal life
in Christ Jesus our Lord.
(Romans 6:23 RSV)

A TREASURED GIFT

There are numerous gifts given us by our God.
He has given us the gift of new life;
And has surrounded us with friends on the roads we trod;
So let us thank and praise Him in the absence of strife!
A treasured gift!

There are numerous gifts given us by our God.
He has given us the gift of genuine love;
And has demonstrated his genuiness by overcoming all odds;
So let us thank and praise Him for leaving his home in heaven above!
A treasured gift!

There are numerous gifts given us by our God.
He has given us the gift of expressive joy;
And has told us that His joy gives strength that we can't dodge;
So let us thank and praise Him while in His employ.
A treasured gift!

There are numerous gifts given us by our God.
He has given us the gift of unwavering faith;
And we cannot please or expect him to affirm with a nod;
So let us thank and praise Him to show we believe
in the Heavenly Estate.
A treasured gift!

Thou wilt keep him in perfect peace whose mind is
stayed on Thee: because he trusteth in Thee.
(Isaiah 26:3 KJV)

PEACE

Our world is in such a troubled state
There seems to be no real peace any place
Thirteen people gunned down for no apparent reason
It appears that some serial killer is having a terrorist season
What has happened to our peace?

Do we not have peace because of our crazy lifestyles?
Do we need to surrender ourselves to the Almighty for a while?
If we really do desire the peace that He gives
We must begin to change the way that we live

Peace, peace, where does it lie?
Voices are calling for peace even as they cry
For loved ones lost by some person badly deranged
But peace will not come until we decide to make a change

Change, you say, just what do you mean?
"May be the situation is not what it may seem."
Just look around you, what do you see?
Evil, disobedience, discontentment, disorder, oppression
And adversity

We need peace in our daily lives
Without peace and tranquility we cannot survive
The conflicts that rage without and within
That causes the inability of our real peace to ever begin

But there is One who can give us lasting peace
If we but trust His Word and on it believe
Follow its teachings and adhere to its laws
And peace will be yours without so many flaws

(Composed on October 7, 2002 following the announcement of the sniper shooting of the 13-year-old Benjamin Tasker Middle School student in Bowie, Maryland.)

Call now; is there any one who will answer you?
To which of the holy ones will you turn?
(Job 5:1 RSV)

For it is written, "He will give his angels charge of you,
to guard you."
(Luke 4:10 RSV)

MY GUARDIAN ANGEL

I have a guardian angel
Who constantly watches over me
He is one on whom I can always depend
He provides outstanding protection
For the many dangers that I fail to see

I have a guardian angel
He carefully guides my feet as I walk
He surrounds me with stamina and strength
This angel guides my tongue and keeps me focused when I talk

I have a guardian angel
He goes ahead of me when I drive
He guides my car in directions of safety
When I'm ready to park I can take great pride

For my guardian angel has gone before me
And selected an adequate parking space
One that I know would not be mine
Were it not for my God's divine grace

My guardian angel was divinely sent
From God's throne in heaven above
He's dispatched for my perfect care and contentment
From a gracious God who is overflowing with kindness and love

My guardian angel stands right by my side
He is there at every single turn
When I might go astray he gently guides
My faltering steps and steadies me so by the fire I am not burned

I praise God for my guardian angel with all of my might
I am so grateful that He is my good friend
I thank God all day and even at night
For my guardian angel who is better than my kin.

See what love the Father has given us, that we
should be called children of God: and so we are.
(1 John 3:3a RSV)

THE LOVE THAT CALLS
US CHILDREN

We live in a world that seems to be so complex.
It is a world on one hand where there are semblances
of genuine love, yet on the other hand, there is the hatred,
the violence. And the crimes, which we seem to inflict on
each other daily. Yet, even with all of the turmoil around us
and topsy-turviness, there is a God who loves us so much
that He calls us children—his sons and daughters. Even
though we tend to go contrary to His will, He never stops
loving us.

It seems that we look for love in all the wrong places. We
try to find it in the fast lanes of life, and in some instances
we are much like the prodigal that Luke describes who looked
in the wrong places, but then decided to return to his Father
Who was eager to respond with participatory love—
with open arms waiting for his return home.

This Scripture in I John can provide great consolation for us
In knowing that the Divine love of the Father was so great
toward us that he adopted us to be His children, His sons
and daughters. And we are His, because He provided for our
atonement through His son Jesus the Christ, so that one day
we could be like Him.

O Lord, our God, we thank you for your steadfast love that you would be willing to call us your children. We want to always be worthy of this great love which you have shown us. Please give us the strength to withstand those evils of the enemy that so often try to beset us. In Jesus' Name, Amen.

Come now, let us reason together, says the Lord:
though your sins are like scarlet, they shall be as
white as snow: though they are red like crimson,
they shall become like wool.
(Isaiah 1:18, RSV)

A MESSAGE OF REDEEMING LOVE

These words speak a most beautiful gospel message.
A message of redeeming love comes through these words—-
not for just a few handpicked individuals, but for the
whole world. It is a world from Gethsemane and Calvary
where the Lamb shed His blood. It is a message of love.
It is a message of hope. It is a message of liberation.

God's ancient people, in their correct rituals, had begun
to forget the real heart of their religion. They had forgotten
to seek justice, to correct oppression, to defend the fatherless,
and to plead for the widow. Isaiah calls them back
to the universality of God's love.

No matter how far we may go from God's will for our
lives, God never gives up on us. God is always ready to
reason with us, and to forgive us. God calls us back to
our brothers and sisters—back to freedom through acts of love.

Merciful God, who has granted us the joy of salvation,
enable us to accept this divine gift with obedience
and gratitude. Amen.

MY PRAYER
(Scriptures)

Blessed is the man who trusts in the Lord,
whose trust is the Lord.
(Jeremiah 17:7 RSV)

"If you love me; you will keep my commandments.
And I will pray the Father, and he will give you another
Counselor, to be with you for ever, even the Spirit of truth,
whom the world cannot receive, because it neither sees
him nor knows him; you know him, for he dwells with you,
and will be in you." "I will not leave you desolate,
I will come to you."
(John 14:15-18 RSV)

Let us hold fast the confession of our hope without wavering,
for he who promised is faithful.
(Hebrews 10:23 RSV)

But this I call to mind, and therefore I have hope:
The steadfast love of the Lord never ceases,
his mercies never come to an end; they are new
every morning; great is thy faithfulness.
(Lamentations 3:21-23 RSV)

For every one who asks receives, and he who seeks finds,
and to him who knocks it will be opened.
(Luke 11:10 RSV)

MY PRAYER

God please bless this day
And may it bring happiness and peace
To all who invest in it without dismay
To make thy divine will to increase

May this day be fruitful and filled with love
A day to give thanks and gratitude to you
Proclaim loyalty and allegiance to the Father above
For his majesty in what he's about to do

God bless this day with your joy
That we may share it with all we meet
As we give a smile without being coy
To all of the pilgrims whom we greet

God bless this day and keep us safe
As we commit ourselves to your care
May we be assured of your bountiful grace
Knowing undoubtedly that you are always there

God bless this day as we forgive
All of those who hurt us along the way
May we ever be conscious that as we live
God expects us to remember those with love when we pray

God bless this day as we go about our work
Giving a full day's work for a full day's pay
At day's end being assured, our duty we did not shirk
And God will be pleased that we did not sway

God please bless this day
And may it bring strength to endure
Whatever we may encounter along the way
As long as thy divine will is assured

My prayer is a prayer for all who take one day at a time
To know unwavering that you are a ruler supreme
No matter where this day takes us, you are a power divine
Who reigns without taking us through the extreme

And my soul shall be joyful in the Lord;
it shall rejoice in his Salvation.
(Psalm 35:9 KJV)

WHAT DO YOU DO WITH DEPRESSION

Do you become depressed some time
even when your life space is filled with joy?
Do you worry more than your share
even when life is sublime?
Do you feel sad even when you
should know the score?

What is it that pierces the recesses of our minds
when all around us is laughter and peace?
Are we overly concerned with things
over which we have no control?
Do you then take a few moments your God to seek?

You might just take a few moments to pray
Ask God who created you to give you a chance
To get on your knees and began to say
That he knows just what you need at a glance

In you, O Lord, I take refuge; let me never be put to shame.
In your righteousness deliver me and rescue me;
incline your ear to me and save me. Be to me a
rock of refuge, a strong fortress, to save me,
for you are my rock and my fortress.
(Psalm 71: 1-3 NRSV)

For God did not give us a spirit of cowardice, but rather a
spirit of power and of love and of self-discipline.
(II Timothy 1:7 NRSV)

FEAR

Whenever my soul becomes gripped by anxiety and fear
I try to remember that God is always near
For He has promised that he would always stay
Close beside me all of the way

And yes, there are times when my spirit gets weak
And I worry about things which seem to me are unique
But when I close my eyes and kneel down to pray
God speaks to my soul without delay

He then leads me to His Holy Word
And as I begin to read, His still, small voice is heard
"For God hath not given us the spirit of fear;
But of power, and of love, and of a sound mind,"
So be of good cheer

I am most grateful to the Almighty for this advice
For His love rids me of anguish, misery and strife
That so often accompanies my inward trepidation
And his power eliminates my intimidation

Fear, dread, panic, terror and alarm
Can cause palpitations, which will bring great harm
To these human bodies that we claim we own
But we can overcome our disquietude with only God alone

So whenever you are burdened down with anxiety and fear
Just remember your Heavenly Father is always near
For he has said in His Holy Word
"I will never leave thee, nor forsake thee..." (Hebrews 13:6b KJV)
And these words you have surely heard.

Blessed are you when people insult, persecute you and
falsely say all kinds of evil against you because of me.
Rejoice and be glad, because great is your reward in heaven,
for in the same way they persecuted the
prophets who were before you.
(Matthew 5: 11-12 NIV)

ARE YOU PERSECUTED?

Persecution is a feeling that is difficult to bear
When persons speak evil against you because of Him is surely not rare
God tells us to rejoice and be exceedingly glad
For your reward in heaven is great, and there is no need to be sad

Persecution is a feeling that causes us to become insulted
People say false things about us and speak evil of all kinds
Our countenance is not one of rejoicing or being glad
Persecution can cause some to become angry and sad

But thank God for His wonderful promises
When we are persecuted falsely for His sake, we will be blessed
We can count on the promises that God makes
We are fortunate to be His children and us He will never forsake

I said, I will watch my ways and keep my tongue from sin.
I will put a muzzle on my mouth as the wicked
are in my presence.
(Psalm 36:1; Proverbs 10:18-20; Matthew 15:1-20; James 3:1-12)

CONTROL THE TONGUE

The tongue must be kept from its sin
Caused many times from what we have within
We need to put muzzles on our mouths
To suppress the terrible things we want to spout

God has commanded us to watch our ways
We can not do this unless we continue to pray
Our strength is really not powerful enough
Unless in God we put our daily trust

The tongue is sometimes very difficult to master
We can't take much criticism, and we are like fire crackers
We want to believe our way is always right
The tongue is always there to enable us to fight

But we must learn to control the tongue before we start
Can we do this without God's help and love in our hearts
I don't think there is the slightest possibility
To put the tongue to rest unless we beg God for His hospitality

O Lord, thou hast searched me, and known me.
Thou knowest my down sitting and mine uprising,
thou understandest my thought afar off.
Thou compassest my path and my lying down and art
acquainted with all my ways. Such knowledge is
too wonderful for me; it is high, I cannot attain unto it.
(Psalm 139: 1-3, 6 KJV)

TAKE SOME TIME FOR YOURSELF

We are all so very busy
Our lives are so full with mostly work and little play
Sometimes our minds become so confused
That we seem not to know how to take a break
Take some time just for yourself

One thing God made very clear, he took a day to take some rest
God's body-spiritual, mental, and physical, being busy with creation
He stopped, took a brief inventory
Decided that all of it was good, but still in the making
God realized that he needed to take some time for himself

It is so wonderful to take time to observe
It is then that we begin to realize
How we have been blessed
When we take a little time to view the mountain peaks
With all of the beautiful green vegetation
We begin to give praise, relax and lose some of our frustration

Today, as I look from my house
My porch faces the golf course
I see so much of what the almighty has created
The beautiful green grass, the flowering trees
The birds flying around singing, and even the bees

The sky is as blue as can be
Here and there, a few white frosty cloud formations
Bring to my mind how as a child
We created so many things mentally from the clouds
Because I'm taking some time for myself
I began to daydream again and use my imagination

As I look, facing the mountain in front of my eyes
The Almighty's closeness in my spirit seems very near
It is the divine presence I begin to feel
And realize it is then the praises overflow in my spirit
For this awesome power is here
Please take some time for yourself

And Jabez called on the God of Israel, saying,
Oh that thou wouldest bless me indeed, and enlarge my coast,
and that thine hand might be with me, and that thou wouldest
keep from evil, that it may not grieve me!
And God granted him that which he requested.
(I Chronicles 4:10 KJV)

I have glorified thee on the earth: I have finished the work
which thou gavest me to do.
(John 17:4 KJV)

Being confident of this very thing, that he which hath begun
a good work in you will perform it until the day of Jesus Christ.
(Philippians 1:6 KJV)

WORK

I admit that being a workaholic
Has never caused me to be ashamed
The work I have done has not even
Brought me great gain
Not yet have I come to be a millionaire
Never really, had even too much to share.

I learned early on in my career
That whatever job God gave me to be
Willing to do it with cheer
To just be very thankful to have a good job
To give each task my very best without ever being a slob.

Believe it or not, I worked for pay since the age of ten
I did not make much money way back then
There were no computers or plasma televisions in my space
But these never kept me from running my race.

Even at the ripe young age of ten
My paycheck was only a smidgen then
It never occurred to me that I wasn't paid much
All I did was clean my third grade teacher's bathroom and such.

I was grateful though to be able to work
Made enough money to buy socks and skirts
Had I made more, my! What could I have done
Tried to help someone else who had none?

In those days money in our home was always scarce
Only dad worked cutting pulpwood to be able to spare
A little food to put on the big wooden table
For a house full of children to help to keep them stable

It was interesting in those days I never knew that I was poor
We had clothes that my Aunt and Uncle sent from up North
Thank God my Mother could sew very well
The clothes were refashioned, and pretty enough to sell.

We all learned that it was good to work
We each had a group of chores that sometimes we tried to shirk
Our parents, were always right there
To provide a little encouragement that wasn't easy to bear—

Sometimes now I wonder how my mother must have felt
There was rarely ever much there for herself
No pretty dresses for Sunday Church or for mother to wear
She made sure each of us had ample clothes fashioned
And made with such care

Mother was a mighty woman, a devout one
Who believed strongly in God
She taught us to love Him with all our hearts as we trod
She prayed with us, and read to us His words
And made very sure
That our love for Him was always very, very pure

Praise be to God today at the wonderful age of seventy three
The work I've done sustained my life wonderfully
At this age I still work hard each blessed day
For being a workaholic is not such a bad or evil way!

To every thing there is a season,
and a time to every purpose under the heaven.
(Ecclesiastes 3:1 KJV)

And that, knowing the time,
that now it is high time to awake out of sleep:
For now is our salvation nearer than when we believed.
(Romans 13:11 KJV)

WHEN I HAVE TIME

When I have the time so many things I'll do to make
life happier and more fair
For those whose lives are crowded now with care;
I'll help to lift them from their low despair
       When I have time.

When I have time the friend I love so well
Shall know no more these weary, toiling days;
I'll lead her feet in pleasant paths always
And cheer her heart with words of sweetest praise.
       When I have time.

When you have time: The friend you hold so dear
May be beyond the reach of all your sweet intent;
May never know that you so kindly meant
To fill her life with sweet content
       When you have time.

Now is the time. Ah friend, no longer wait
To scatter loving smiles and words of cheer
To those around whose lives are now so dear
They may not need you in the coming year
      Now is the time

The thoughts of the righteous are right:
but the counsels of the wicked are deceit.
(Proverbs 12:5 KJV)

Wherefore seeing we also are compassed about with so great
a cloud of witnesses, let us lay aside every weight,
and the sin, which doth so easily beset us, and let us run
with patience the race that is set before us, Looking unto
Jesus the author and finisher of our faith; who for the joy
that was set before him endured the cross, despising the shame,
and is set down at the right hand of the throne of God.
(Hebrews 12:1-2 KJV)

NEW YEAR'S RESOLUTIONS

What New Year's resolutions will you make this year 2002?
Did you make them in the precious name of the Father and the Son?
Or did you just make your trite promises in your own powerless name
Remember now when the resolutions are broken
It will be only to your shame

Some people say they don't make New Year's resolutions
The reason that they cannot keep them from becoming an intrusion
So they continue to do things in the same old way
Fighting battles with the devil every single day

People tend to bemoan all the mishaps that Satan causes
They fail to even consider all their other many pauses
That keeps them shackled and completely bound
To an evil, destructive force that looms all around

There is nothing wrong with making resolutions
prior to New Year's Day
We all need some well thought out plans to portray
To others who may be struggling to make their life better
You can be an example for these no matter what the weather

What we all need to do is pray to the God we serve
To enable us to always have the kind of reserve
To just continually do the right thing
And rely on God's enabling help our success He will bring

African-American History
(Scriptures)

Hear instruction and be wise, and do not neglect it
(Proverbs 8:33 RSV)

Therefore also the Wisdom of God said, 'I will send them
prophets and apostles, some of whom they will kill and perse-
cute,' that the blood of all the prophets, shed from the foundation
of the world, may be required of this generation, from the
blood of Abel to the blood of Zechariah who perished
between the altar and the sanctuary. Yes, I tell you,
it shall be required of this generation.
(Luke 11: 49-51 RSV)

African-American History

We celebrate African-American history one month of the year;
One month is not enough time to bring us great cheer.
It's not enough to enumerate all the accomplishments we have made:
Especially those omitted from the history books when we were slaves.

It is one's history, which is a great source of joy and pride;
Ours was kept from us to prevent great strides;
In imitating those who had gone on before;
And who could have colored the history books by the score.

Yet, for the most part, it was as if we didn't exist;
Just a little was written between and betwixt;
The pages of all American history books;
As if the only thing we knew how to do was to cook.

But if anyone would research the anals of slavery and other times past;
They would find that African-Americans made significant
contributions that last and last
These were not all made in just song and dance.
But in literature, in science, art, in sports, and many more if given
the chance.

There were so many times we were just held back;
And this was only because our skin was black
We did well to have been educated in one-room schools;
Most times without ever having the proper tools.

Interestingly enough some did complain;
But it certainly was not to their gain;

For many who complained just lost their life;
At the hands of some person who was filled with strife.

Some were constantly ridiculed with intimidation;
While others were beaten and filled with trepidation
It was terrible to have to live in this kind of shame
Because persons thought we might rise up against them
and cause them pain.

As a child, I grew up in a little town in the South;
My mother taught us to always watch the mouth;
"Be Careful what you say to anybody you meet;"
"And especially those people you meet downtown
on the street."

I thank God today that Jesus taught us to forgive;
Whoever wronged us as long as we live;
We pray daily for justice to always prevail;
In the lives of our future generation both male and female.

So let us follow the example that Jesus taught;
And continue to push for the dream that Dr. King sought;
That one day our little boys and our precious little girls;
Will find their rightful place within this beautiful world.

Then David said to Solomon his son,
"Be strong, take heart, and do
it; never be daunted or dismayed, for the Eternal your
God, even my God, is with you; he will never fail
you nor forsake you before all the work needed for the
temple of the Eternal is finished."
(I Chronicles 28:20 TJMB)

He has showed you, O man, what is good;
and what does the Lord
require of you but to do justice, and to love kindness and
to walk humbly with your God?
(Micah 6:8 RSV)

Now to him who is able to strengthen you according to my
gospel and the preaching of Jesus Christ, according to the
revelation of the mystery which was kept secret for long ages
(Romans 16:25 RSV)

STRONG BLACK WOMAN!

Black woman, yes you are strong
Can hear it as you sing your songs
Can feel it every time you speak
Surely knew it when you preached

Black woman, yes you are strong
Can see you and know you belong
Active in anything in this world
As things in the home continue to unfurl

Black woman, yes you are strong
Can see you working all day long
Rarely ever stopping to take a rest
Nursing your children from your breast

Black woman, yes you are strong
Protecting your family from all harm
Caring for children, keeping them clean
Encouraging them not to ever be mean

Black woman, yes you are strong
We appreciate your kindness and your bond
We love you strong sistas even as we weep
For we know your stress and your belief
Black Woman, stay strong!

Happy the man who never goes by the advice of the ungodly,
who never takes the sinners' road, nor joins the
company of scoffers, but finds his joy in the Eternal's law,
poring over it day and night.
(Psalms 1:1 TJMB)

STRONG MEN

Strong men are rough and durable,
Firm and lasting, endeared with love,
Deep, unconditional not too afraid to cry and
With disappointments and tragedies as peaceful as a dove

Strong men are excellent lovers
Of God, family and friends
They are our Nation's continued warriors
On whom we can certainly depend

Strong men are willing to provide
As they work so many hours
To give much more than is required
So their families are healthy and empowered

Strong men are caring, thoughtful
They remember special days with appropriate cards and gifts
Without having to be reminded
They show appreciation even amid the shifts

Strong men are helpful and saturated with faith
In those with whom he shares
Although they may not make it without God's grace
Strong men are forgiving and willing to bear

Strong men are a wonderful commodity
To always have around
They can clean, wash and cook; absolutely!
To this, we should certainly give a starry crown!

The man called his wife's name Eve,
because she was the mother of all living.
(Genesis 3:20 RSV)

But we were gentle among you,
like a nurse taking care of her children.
(I Thessalonians 2:7 RSV)

For God so loved the world, that he gave his only begotten son;
that whosoever believeth in him should not perish,
but have everlasting life.
(John 3: 16 RSV)

I REMEMBER MOTHER

Although it has been a long, long time
Since my mother moved to her home sublime
I still remember the teachings she taught
They were so superb and great riches they have brought

I remember all of those old hymns she used to sing
Like "The Old Rugged Cross," that even now it brings
The greatest comfort to my troubled soul
In those dark moments of my life when disappointments roll

I remember how she taught me to read
When I would stand firmly between her knees
And mother would syllabicate each word two or three times
From "The Old Woman In The Shoe" until firmly indelible in my mind

I remember too how mother taught us how to clean
And in that department, we thought she was being very mean
But now when I reminiscence on then and today
I realize how important these teachings were that we would not sway

For when I am confronted with cleaning my own home
It is not as difficult now because I was taught that "Your house
Is your throne"
This meant to mother that we were Kings and Queens
She often told us this to help build our self-esteem

And build our self-esteem-My! My! She did a magnificent job
Mother prepared us for the vicissitudes of the life we would trod
For there were many days that we would experience put downs
No matter how excellent and perfect we performed our rounds

I remember mother, who read the Bible to us each day
I remember mother calling us to join her on her knees to pray
I remember mother as she taught us how to meditate
On the Holy Bible, its words helped to consecrate

In teaching of the Bible Mother was very wise
I remember her pointing out verses for us to memorize
She reminded us that all of our memory skills were gifts from above
A verse like John 3:16 to teach us about God's unconditional love

I will always remember the things my mother taught
They have been so crucial in the way God has wrought
In enabling each of us to love and care about each other
And although our family has dwindled we love each sister and brother
I will always remember mother!

Then Adam named his wife Eve,
because she would be the mother of all people everywhere
(Genesis 3:20 NLT)

MOTHERS

Mothers are such wonderful people
Some of them work day and night
They tend to forget about themselves
They are an excellent example of doing things right

We don't realize what our mothers go through
Their days are so long-they cook, wash, clean and more
They never seem to know how to stop
There is so much to do because of their chores

Good mothers are kind and exemplify love
They teach us so much about scriptures so sacred and true
Mothers are gifts from an everlasting, merciful God above
We need to appreciate mothers peacefulness-her talk is rather smooth

Mothers should be remembered every single day
We remember their prayers and their songs
Mothers should be remembered for the way they pray
To open shut doors for us, and for us to become strong

My son, obey your father's commands, and don't neglect your mother's teaching. Keep their words always in your heart. Tie them around your neck. Wherever you walk, their counsel can lead you. When you sleep, they will protect you. When you wake up in the morning, they will advise you. For these commands and this teaching is a lamp to light the way ahead of you. The correction of discipline is the way of life.
(Proverbs 6:20-23 NLT)

MY FATHER

My father was a very strong man and very good
Who loved his big family and provided for us the best he could
Food supply was very scarce on some days
Only because my father received little in terms of his wages

Dad always had a beautiful garden
Where lots of leafy vegetables grew
Although he suffered from painful cramps in his hands
He still plowed and kept his garden like a man

The only job available for my father was to cut pulpwood
And this was the job in which he engaged
Holding a saw all day to cut wood caused much pain
But my father cut wood each day unless there was rain

*My Child, keep your father's commandment, and do not
forsake your mother's teaching. Bind them upon your
heart always; tie them around your neck.*
(Proverbs 6:20-21 NRSV)

*Then were there brought unto him little children, that he should
Put his hands on them, and pray; and the disciples rebuked them.
But Jesus said, Suffer little children, and forbid them not, to
come unto me; for of such is the kingdom of heaven.
And he laid his hands on them and departed thence.*
(Matthew 19:13-15 KJV)

CHILDREN

Children are God's great blessing to us,
We are so grateful for their innocent trust;
That we need to live our very best,
So that we can always stand their test.

This means we must take the right stand,
It means we always try to keep God's command,
We must strive diligently to do what is right;
So that what we do will be pleasing in God's sight.

Biological children are not the only ones we cherish
Those in our community and the world we must add to our measure
We can teach them the way they should grow and go;
And constantly remind them that God loves them so.

We should never one of these precious souls mistreat,
Be careful my friends, with each little one we meet,
Speak a kind word of encouragement, love and joy;
To make each day happier than the day before.

For these little children are jewels from God
Given to us to nurture as along life's roads we trod.
So let us treat them gently, kind and sweet;
As if they were our pearls and diamonds about
which we must be discreet.

Children are God's great blessings to us,
They are ours to guide, to love, to teach, to trust,
All that we know about God's unconditional love,
That always comes from the Father above.

Then great blessings from God we shall receive;
We can watch them grow and in themselves believe;
That in His providence eternal life He will provide;
If they follow and obey his teaching, they can survive

So, please let all of us love the children unconditionally!

And he took a child, and set him in the midst of them:
and when he had taken him in his arms, he said unto them.
(Mark 9:36 KJV)

Children obey your parents in all things:
for this is well pleasing unto the Lord.
(Colossians 3:20 KJV)

MY CHILDREN

I give praise to the God above
For giving me three adorable children to love
They are so precious to our family
Their love for each other shows so bountifully

One of the things that brings great joy
Is to know that your child loves the Lord
It's easy to see because they demonstrate it fully
In the way they serve God without being unruly

They are up and out to church each Sunday
And they practice what they're taught on Monday
Their children always they take
To church on Sunday without a break

No, perfect they are not just yet
But for perfection they strive to get
They love you God, and it makes us proud
To know they try to worship, praise
And serve you without a doubt

Every good gift and every perfect gift is from above,
and cometh down from the
Father of lights, with who is no variableness,
neither shadow of twining.
(James 1:17 KJV)

MY CHILDREN
(Poem I)

My children are like sparkling diamonds
They are God's precious jewels to me
I constantly praise Him and give Him the glory
For these three invaluable gifts whom I love unconditionally

First, is the eldest—a daughter He gave
Who blesses my soul with her caring and pleasant smile
She shares with me like a sister would
From whom I have always learned to "do the right thing"
By every child

She has an extraordinary love for children
Evidenced by her love and compassionate concern
That she provides for every child she meets
She continually gives of herself unstintingly as her love is
confirmed

She was named for one of my cousins
A name that I could never forget
Even before she was delivered from my womb
The name was ingrained in my mind, the beautiful name,
Linette

Music is one of her great loves
From almost infancy she has sung her part
She loves to play the piano and sing
This brings great joy to everyone's heart

Every good gift and every perfect gift is from above,
and cometh down from the
Father of lights, with whom is no variableness,
neither shadow of twining.
(James 1:17 KJV)

MY CHILDREN
My Second Child
(Poem II)

My second eldest child is a blessing for sure
Another diamond, and a singing son
We must praise God for these innate talents
Which he now has devoted to whom they really belong

This first son, we gave his father's name
It turned out to be an excellent choice
Now that he's an adult we see his father's ways and likeness
And he and his father are much the same

He is a man of many words some times
At others he is reserved and very quiet
But whenever he does decide to speak
His words are listened too and he is a riot

Singing is a marvelous talent from God
This talent his father did not possess
But we named this son Joseph, Jr.
And many, many persons have been really blessed

Blessed by his singing the songs of Zion
Blessed by his sincere prayers divine
Blessed by his special love for God and his entire family
Blessed by the way he lets his light so shine

Every good gift and every perfect gift is from above,
and cometh down from the
Father of lights, with whom is no variableness,
neither shadow of twining.
(James 1:17 KJV)

MY CHILDREN
My Third Child
(Poem III)

My third and youngest child is another diamond from God
A teaser from the very depths of his soul
He deeply loves God and his family
And they really respect his goals

He is such a gifted young man
Whose colorful art adorns our home
He too, loves to make melodious music
He sings, direct choirs, and with gifts of service has really grown

He, like the others, loves the Lord
His dedication to church work, I commend
He is a person who speaks his mind
But has a beautiful spirit inspired by a grin

We named this youngest of these three—Alvin Bernard
For one of my brothers, because you see
When so many times, I had a great need
Alvin was always there for me

Bernard, as we refer to this youngest child
Loves to drive and ride in unique style
He has a story that he usually tells with a smile
About his reason for riding each and every mile

I really thank God for the jewels of mine
They have brought me great sunshine
Even amid the storms and the rain
They have brought joy to my spirit over and over again

As for me, I am weak and wretched; O God, make haste to me.
Thou art my help and my deliverer; tarry not O Eternal.
(Psalm 70:5 TJMB)

This is what I command you, to love one another.
(John 15:17 TJMB)

GRANDPARENTS

There are times in our lives
When we need a helping hand
There are times in our lives
When we need friends who understand
That's when God sends grandparents along!

There are times in our lives
When there are pains of frustration and doubt
There are times in our lives
When faith is shattered all about
That's when God sends grandparents along!

Thank you, dear God for grandparents today
Thank you for the love they share
Thank you for the tower of strength they display
Thank you for we know they really care
Praise your name for sending Grandparents our way!

When I call to remembrance the unfeigned faith
That is in thee, which dwelt first in thy grandmother
Lois, and thy mother Eunice; and I am
persuaded that in thee also.
(II Timothy 1:5 KJV)

GRANDPARENTS, GOD'S GIFT

What a great gift God gave
When He let us have grandparents who help and care
What a blessing they are to help us save
Our souls from sin as we share
Lives with Jesus full and free
Serving a God with grace sufficient for Thee

So grandparents, as we celebrate today
We salute all of you with love, peace and joy
We pray God will ever bless you along the way
Because you are very special in God's employ
In helping to bring God's kingdom for all
That we who love you may never stumble or fall

As the Father knoweth me, even so know I the Father:
And I lay down my life for the sheep.
(John 10:15 KJV)

Many are the afflictions of the righteous:
but the Lord delivereth him out of them all.
(Psalm 34:19 KJV)

Jalen- On Life

We know that life is a precious commodity;
With the breath to breathe into being throughout eternity
From birth, physicians knew Jalen's life would be hard
He would require several miracles from an almighty God.

Although he has been a frequent patient in intensive care;
There is never a doubt that the miracle is there.
Life is a miracle, as some of us know;
And God intervened in Jalen's
In order that he could continue to grow.

My! What a beautiful smile always adorns Jalen's face.
His dimples are a reminder of God's everlasting grace;
To a little child who had an innate desire to live;
And to parents who have given all the care any one could
Be expected to give.

Jalen's father made the hospital his home;
And made a vow never to leave him alone,
Until the critical time of his illness had passed
And Jalen could return to his home at last.

Jalen's mom, grandparents, great grand parents
And godparents and other family stood by his side
With prayers in adherence to God's will
Anointing with oil, hugs and kisses
While physicians and nurse marveled at Jalen's
Unrelenting will to live.

With a collapsed esophagus Jalen was born
And his food intake could not follow the norm
Feedings through tubes was not Jalen's style
So his hands found a way to pull out the tube after awhile

When a medical procedure to correct the problem was announced
Jalen's weight only stood at a few ounces,
But what a miracle of strength God has given this little boy.
The procedure's success gave us all a bundle of joy!

Jalen is not completely well, but a happy child is he!
He can take regular feedings during the day
and they are more than three.
Then at night they are supplemented with feeding from the tube
At this writing he has gained almost eight pounds,
And he surely does not suffer from the blues

I believe if Jalen could say more than "da da" or "bye bye"
He would constantly look up to the beautiful blue sky
And sing praises to the almighty Father above
For his compassionate healing care and his undying love

(On January 11, 2003, Jalen celebrated his third birthday with a party
at Chuckie Cheese.His mom brought him from NY to DC for the
party. He still cannot eat most things but he is healthy with his night
feedings and day feedings of baby foods he is still a very happy child)

Greater love hath no man than this,
that a man lay down his life for his friend.
(John 15:13 KJV)

MY FRIEND

There's nothing like having a friend with whom to share
All of life's burdens, joys, blessings and care
Their joy, the humor, the laughter they provide
Cause all of my trials and tribulations to subside.

This friend of mine is like medicine sublime
She's like nourishment to the psyche when the sun doesn't shine
This friend of mine is like a very precious stone
With its value, its glitter, and the way it stands out all alone.

This friend of mine brings joy to all she meets
Her humorous attitude is always there to greet
Each person who comes along her path
She has a passion to make them laugh.

My friend has a very giving heart
Whatever she has, she wants to share a part
Her desire is to bring happiness each and every day
To all of her friends and neighbors who pass her way

Wouldn't you like to have a friend like mine?
A friend who is always loving and kind?
I believe your answer is yes, you see
Because my friend is one who has been set free!

(This poem is dedicated to my good friend Virginia Schuyler Waddy)

*Tomorrow about this time I will send to you a man from
the land of Benjamin, and you shall anoint him to be prince
over my people Israel. He shall save my people from the
hand of the Philistines; for I have seen the affliction of
my people, because their cry has come to me.*
(I Samuel 9:16 RSV)

*For this is the message which you have heard from the
beginning, that we should love one another, and not be like Cain,
who was of the evil one and murdered his brother.
And why did he murder him? Because his own deeds
were evil and his brother's righteous. Do not wonder,
brethren, that the world hates you. We know that we have
passed out of death into life, because we love the brethren.
He who does not love abides in death.*
(I John 3: 11-14 RSV)

SOUNDING THE ALARM

Today, we observe World AIDS Day
To call attention to the fact
That so many of our people suffer from HIV and AIDS
And we continue to be silent as we give God praise
So today we are sounding the alarm!

So today, I am calling to the task
Clergy—Pastors, Bishops, Associate Ministers, Assistant Ministers,
Youth Ministers, and all those who are willing to unmask
The hesitation and procrastination that we seem to ignore
Of HIV and AIDS that continually knocks on our doors.
We are sounding the alarm!

We can no longer sit silently and not get involved
We must put on God's armor and try to resolve
This dreaded disease that wrecks havoc in
the African American Community
We must do this together in Christian Unity.
So join us in sounding the alarm!

This battle does not belong to one woman or one man
It's a battle where every Christian needs to take a stand
And put all of our idiosyncrasies aside
And begin to fight the fight as we in God abide
We are sounding the alarm!

Some how we tend to think that we have eradicated HIV/AIDS
But statistically it is still very much on the rage
Immobilizing many of our people one by one
We cannot stop fighting until the battle is completely won
We are sounding the alarm!

Our women, men and even our children
Are bearing heavy burdens from the decay of their immune system
So let's come together when we receive the call
And join in this battle one and all
We are sounding the alarm!

Remember, in this community in the year of our Lord 1998
We came together at New Hope to try to set the record straight
Providing information, knowledge and skills ability
So we'd be more informed and could react responsibly
Again, we are sounding the alarm!

That was fourteen years ago, my friends
We have been working very hard ever since then
To enable you to fully understand
That it's not about the how, but how we can
eradicate on every hand
We are sounding the alarm!

So please join us in this tremendous fight
We need to begin to set things aright
Much of fourteen years, we have not yielded to the call
In this year 2002, we are standing on the wall
To sound the alarm loudly for all of you my friends

Please won't you help us save this generation and those to come
from having to try to live with HIV/AIDS?

AIDS AND THE CHURCH
(Scriptures)

Fear not, stand firm, and see the salvation of the Lord, which he will work for you today; for the Egyptians whom you see today, you shall never see again.
(Exodus 14:13 RSV)

Fear Not, for I am with you, be not dismayed, for I am your God; I will strengthen you, I will help you, I will uphold you with my victorious right hand.
(Isaiah 41:10 RSV)

These things I have spoken unto you, that in me ye might have peace. In the world ye shall have tribulation; but be of good cheer; I have overcome the world.
(John 16:33 KJV)

Casting all your care upon him; for he careth for you.
(I Peter 5:7 KJV)

AIDS AND THE CHURCH

Oh church founded by Christ, why are you so fearful
Within your walls you were founded to set the captives free
But you have neglected those who need you the most
You have looked in other directions, is it because
you did not wish to see?
Those who are bound by HIV?
AIDS and the church!

Jesus said over two thousands years ago of the
church that he had built
"On this rock I will build my church and the gates of hell
shall not prevail against it."

But the rock, the very foundation of the church is warbling
Satan, that evil spirit, is trying desperately to prevail
against the church
He would have you think to help those with
AIDS is downright against God's perfect will
But let me encourage you that Satan is the
Father of liars, He will not be ever still

Believe me, that AIDS epidemic is a tragic problem
of this 21st Century
And the church is very lax in addressing this formidable need
Did not Jesus heal the lepers? The brokenhearted, free the captives,
And gave sight to the blind? What makes you think
that you are following
God's commands? When you and your leaders refuse to
lend a helping hand
AIDS and the Church!

Whenever Jesus encountered someone in bondage with a malady
Hesitation was never a problem for Him
He did not question how the individual acquired the disease
But he sought quickly to bring them some kind of relief
Jesus prayed; he touched; he wrote on the ground; he mixed spit
With clay, He asked questions, but he never condemned
Why can't the church try to be more compassionate, like Him?
AIDS and the Church!

Oh church, how long will we hesitate to become involved
In the healing of God's people who are hurting
from HIV and AIDS?
Clergy, how long will our children, our daughters,
our mothers, and our
Grandmothers and our fathers and brothers die
from this dreaded pandemic
While like Pilate, we just sit by and try to
wash the guilt from our hands
While God is calling with a loud voice from all over this land
For you clergy, to provide the balm from Gilead
For the healing of our people who are constantly sick and sad
AIDS and the Church!

Remember those that are in bonds as bound with them;
and them which suffer adversity as being yourselves in the body.
(AKJV)

MY HIV/AIDS SUPPORT GROUP
(Fluvanna Correctional Center
for Women)

God blesses us until the blessings overflow;
Many blessings are too innumerable to count
But one of these is my HIV/AIDS Support Group
In amazement, I observe their growth
Each week as I listen attentively to the situations they surmount

In this group of women inmates, one can certainly find
Persons who are not afraid to express the way they feel
To someone who will listen with a compassionate mind
And one who is willing constantly to be for "real."

One significant thing about these women is
They are very eager to learn
As much as they can about this dreaded disease
My HIV/AIDS Support Group is very quick to discern
All are not infected, but affected by some they do not
wish to displease

Each week when the signing in their names is past
And an inmate volunteer is needed to pray
Thanks be to God, no votes have to be cast
From one of the women an offer is made

These prayers so earnestly and reverently prayed
Will bring joy to hear, and tears to your eyes
When they remember families, and especially their
Children without delay
It is no wonder these devoted mothers cry

And yes, they realize they have made serious mistakes
But they want to try to make the best of the situation
They all look forward to the time when this cycle they can break
And join their families in love, joy and reconciliation

And Isaiah said, Take a lump of figs. And they took
and laid it on the boil, and he recovered.
(II Kings 20:7 KJV)

I will never forget thy precepts:
for with them thou hast quickened me.
(Psalm 119:93 KJV)

And when he had looked round about on them with anger,
being grieved for the hardness of their hearts, he saith unto
the man, Stretch forth thine hand. And he stretched it out:
and his hand was restored whole as the other.
(Mark 3:5 KJV)

PAIN

There is a pain I feel deep down inside
For those around this world who did not abide
In the faith hope and love of Jesus the Christ
Who suffered, bled, died and arose for our eternal life

This Pain stirs my heart and mind sometimes so
That it causes me to tremble because I know
That those who are bound by sin and shame
Must Repent, receive Jesus as Savior
And be reborn in His Name

The pain I speak of is not necessarily physical pain
It is a deep depressive hurt that I cannot fully explain
But I can certainly tell you about the joy of the Lord
As we spread happiness and peace freely aboard

Today is the day that the Lord has made
A day especially for you to keep your mind staid
On Jesus the Savior who can redeem your soul
Just accept him today and He will make you whole.

Love is patient; love is kind; love is not envious or boastful
Or arrogant or rude. It does not insist on its own way;
it is not irritable or resentful; it does not rejoice in wrongdoing,
but rejoices in the truth. It hears all things, believes all things,
hopes all things, endures all things. Love never ends.
But as for prophecies, they will come to an end;
as for tongues, they will cease; as for knowledge,
it will come to an end. And now faith, hope and love abide,
these three; and the greatest of these is love.
(I Cor. 13:4-8; 13:13)

A TRIBUTE TO SHERRELL FROM MAMA

Sherrell, my love for you will never, never die
The thoughts of your suffering still make me cry
But, I tried to help you manage your pain
And now, I'm aware that heaven is the gain.

I remember your kind and gracious way
Of letting me be aware by just what you would say
About my care, nurture and unconditional love for you
As God's love, strength and blessing brought me through.

Had I not had God right by my side
I could not have made it when you died
Because I felt a part of me had left me stunned
And I am aware it will take some time to overcome

I thank the doctors, nurses and staff at UVA
For their unstinting care that they always gave
Especially, I thank "Peter" my guardian angel, heaven sent
For his understanding, compassion, caring and encouragement

I'll miss your beautiful smile and loving touch
I'll miss the conversation we shared so much
I'll miss the kindness you always knew how to show
I'll miss seeing your lovely face always aglow.

Thank you God for the memories.

They that wait upon the Lord shall renew their strength;
they shall mount up with wings as eagles; they shall run,
and not be weary; and they shall walk, and not faint.
(Isaiah 40:31 KJV)

MEMORIES

IN HONOR OF THE MEMORY
OF MILTON SMITH

When we lose someone we love just in the prime of their years,
It is just a natural, human response to shed many, many silent tears,
There are so many things about love that we just didn't get to say
And we begin to blame ourselves for the many ways we drifted away.

We always thought that there would have been plenty of time,
To make amends for situations which could have been more kind.
But here we are today feeling weary, worn, and very sad,
Because the time slipped away,
but thanks for memories that make us glad.

We are here today because of these memories—
of our father and our brother,
In our hearts and minds thinking about "Poochie"-
There will never be another.
One who was always a joy to his children, family and to his friends
And even to "Storm" who would look
and wait for him until the very end.

Hardy Drive will probably never be quite the same without him.
Who was always loving, kind, jovial,
and filled with music to the brim.
When he set his mind to dancing the "slop,"
he was an expert that no one could beat
In fact, "Sis" has been known to tell others that he had "magic feet."

While I realize that there is nothing quite so
difficult to overcome as grief,
Take these memories and rejoice in your laughter as you think of
"Poochie's magic feet,
Remember: "My love won't hurt Anybody,
but I just want to mend your broken heart,"
Think on all of these memories, start to renew your life,
 and then begin to chart,
A life with the Father, the Son Jesus the Christ, and The Holy Spirit
And let them all become a part!

ORDER INFORMATION

_____YES, I want_____copies of
MY SOUL EXPLODES
Praise and Meditation Thoughts

For $12.95 each

Please include $1.95 shipping and handling for one book,
and $1.00 for each additional book.

Virginia residents must include 4.5% sales tax.

Name _____

Address_____

City_____State____ Zip_____

Phone_____E-Mail_____

Amount Enclosed $ _____

Payment must accompany orders. Allow three weeks for delivery.

Make checks/Money Orders payable to Dr. Nan M. Brown

Send to:

Brown Publishing
Post Office Box 39
Kents Store, Virginia 23084

ORDER INFORMATION

_____YES, I want_____copies of
MY SOUL EXPLODES
Praise and Meditation Thoughts

For $12.95 each

Please include $1.95 shipping and handling for one book,
and $1.00 for each additional book.

Virginia residents must include 4.5% sales tax.

Name _____

Address_____

City_____State____ Zip_____

Phone_____E-Mail_____

Amount Enclosed $ _____

Payment must accompany orders. Allow three weeks for delivery.

Make checks/Money Orders payable to Dr. Nan M. Brown

Send to:

Brown Publishing
Post Office Box 39
Kents Store, Virginia 23084